Beautiful Oregon

BEAUTIFUL WEST PUBLISHING COMPANY

CURRENT BOOKS

Mt. Hood, Montana, Utah, Oregon, Washington, California, Northern California, Colorado, Hawaii, Alaska, Western Impressions, 25 Oregon Weekend Adventures, and photographic prints and placemats.

FORTHCOMING BOOKS

Maryland, Georgia, New York, Virginia, Arizona, New Mexico, California Missions, San Francisco, Lewis and Clark Country, Sierra Nevada, Oregon Coast, Southern California, Mexico.

Send for complete catalog, 50¢

Beautiful West Publishing Company
202 N.W. 21st Avenue ● Portland, Oregon, 97209

Beautiful Oregon

Featuring RAY ATKESON Photography

Text by Paul M. Lewis

Fourth Edition, Revised

Copyright © 1976 by Beautiful Oregon Publications, Inc.
All rights reserved.
Robert D. Shangle, Publisher
First Edition Published 1974, Second Edition 1976
ISBN 0-915796-01-5 (paperback)
ISBN 0-915796-10-4 (hardbound)
Printed in the United States of America

RAY ATKESON

Ray Atkeson has photographed Oregon and the Pacific Northwest for more than thirty years. He was born in the Midwest and spent his early years in Illinois and Missouri. So the Northwest is all the more exciting to him for the comparisons he is able to draw with other areas.

When he moved to the Northwest he became a photographer for a commercial studio in Portland. On weekends he roamed the Northwest with his camera. His early work was purchased by national publications and newspapers such as The New York Times, The Kansas City Star, The Houston Chronicle, and The London Illustrated News.

Since 1946 his work has appeared frequently in Holiday, Time, Sports Illustrated, National Geographic, and many other publications of national and international reputation.

His enthusiasm for mountaineering and the outdoors adds that extra dimension that raises his portraits of nature to the highest level of interpretative art.

CONTENTS

Beautiful Oregon

MEN have a great need to know that there are still places on this earth that can honestly be called wild and unspoiled. We have been made aware in the past few years that the thrust of man's technology is reaching into and causing great havoc in those realms of nature up to recent times free from our wholesale and presumptuous tampering. We who were intended to be congenial participants in nature's "planned" society have become wastrels and despoilers, like wanton children, of the bounty lavished on us by an orderly natural system. It is not just exaggerated rhetoric to say that lives and living space may before long be as programmed and regimented as those Orwell imagined in his frightening vision of the future. But we seem at last to be facing up to what we have wrought, making efforts to find and preserve the Shangri-la's still remaining, those still-magical places "progress" has not reached.

There must still be places in our world where nature has been allowed to hold on to some of her secrets. Deep in the wilderness, where it still exists, we can experience the unknowable, and momentarily transcend our own limitations. This, in human terms, is the *only* progress. When we enter the earth's wild sanctuaries we can reach out and stretch our souls. Among the privileged regions of our world where we can still find these hideaways is one in our own country marked out both by political and natural boundaries, the place called "Oregon."

In recent times, Oregon has achieved a degree of standing in the nation, and elsewhere, as a place occupied by people who care about staying on the best terms with the plant and animal life of which they are a part. So Oregon is more than a state; it is, indeed, a state of mind. Here the theatre of the wilderness is not only a living presence, but its audience is becoming more and more aware of the permanent values that attach to the appreciation of a fragile and all too impermanent beauty.

The abundantly varied settings within the borders of Oregon have been attested to by all who have experienced them and have been able to express that experience in some way. Vivid contrasts are dictated by the two main natural systems that control Oregon's land, skies, and waters: the Pacific Ocean and the Cascade Range. The jagged mountain barrier slices into the skies from north to south, cutting off the western third of the state from the eastern two-thirds. Result: west of the mountains lavish rain that rides in on Pacific storm systems as far as the Cascade ridge; on the east side, minimal rainfall from the much-weakened cloud systems that get past the Cascade sentinels.

The rain that falls blessedly and abundantly on western Oregon has occasioned, at times, some corner-of-the-mouth comments by a few transplanted transgressors who unaccountably object to being rain-dampened when they go for a swim in a lake or the ocean. Oregon rain is both symbol and source of the regeneration of living things. Without so much of it the descriptive, "spectacular," could not be applied to the wild rivers with their abundant fish life, the endless forests of fir and pine, the dazzling and pervasive green ambiance of even the urban areas, the brilliant and stately rhododendrons that grow in such profusion. Oregon's rain is nearly always gentle. Its caress can magically release the sweet forest aromas when the spell of a dry summer is first broken. Standing in a cedar grove just recently visited by rain, a forest visitor breathes a scent whose fragrant mix remains long afterwards in his memory.

The rainy third of Oregon is well known. But across the mountains the land is higher and drier, in addition to being less publicized. This region provides a startling contrast to the western part in appearance and way of life, and, of course, in geological history. The southeastern section is predominantly a desert, with ghost towns and bizarre rock formations. In this fossil-rich area, history is measured in non-human terms.

In one of the preceding paragraphs it was mentioned that Oregonians are aware of what they have and that they are bent on preserving it. This may have implied a Pollyanna picture of Goodness clad in shining raiment, with maybe a halo for added effect. That was not the intention, and a disclaimer should probably be inserted here, but one that leaves the primary point intact. Oregon, it can be said, has only a small share of those who rape its lands and foul its air and water. But these destructive elements are no longer regarded (if they ever were) as inevitable accompaniments of civilization. Oregon has long been and still is a leader in the efforts to reverse man's depredations upon the world around him. In the pages that follow you will see symbolic evidence of how well Oregon citizens have succeeded in preserving the fragile beauty surrounding them. The sensitive photographic portraits of Ray Atkeson interpret the many moods and faces of nature frolicking unhindered on the Oregon stage.

The book also pays some attention to the works of the human participants, but these are always set against the backdrop of nature's greater drama. This is as it should be, for nearly all of Oregon's big and little towns owe their acqaintance with the good life to matchless settings provided by a prodigal nature. One brilliant example of this is found in the southern Oregon town of Ashland. There, the Oregon Shakespearean Festival, a world-famous summer celebration of the Bard, is held in an outdoor Elizabethan theatre, enfolded in an incomparable setting enhanced by man's appreciative art.

In the 1850s, Theodore Winthrop (a descendant of John Winthrop of the Massachusetts Bay Colony) traveled around the Northwest and wrote about the region. It was his vision that the people of Oregon would bring the American idea to a greater realization by eliminating the worst of Old World civilization and by creating "new habits of life and thought." One might surmise with some justification that the happy relationship Oregonians are establishing with their environment is a result of those "new habits," fostered by some mysterious process of reciprocity. If Oregon remains one of the places where large areas are left in their natural state or nearly so, it will happen because the people here, having the power to do environmental good or evil, will have chosen the former course, in the knowledge that their action has preserved a means of human renewal and reinvigoration.

PHOTO DESCRIPTIONS

Listed below are descriptions of all full-page and two-page pictures not otherwise identified.

(Front cover) CRATER LAKE ... Wizard Island, an extinct volcanic cone which formed on the floor of Crater Lake 2,000 feet below the surface of the water, seemingly floats on the beautiful blue lake.

(Page 9) EAGLE CREEK PUNCH BOWL ... Indian summer haze veils the beautiful Eagle Creek Punch Bowl, reached by a scenic trail in the Mt. Hood National Forest.

(Page 12 & 13) COLUMBIA RIVER GORGE ... Green fields of a farm and golden tints of autumn make the famed Columbia River Gorge even more beautiful than usual. This view was photographed from the scenic Columbia River Highway in Oregon.

(Pages 14 & 15) OREGON COAST ... Picturesque weather-sculptured trees in Ecola State Park frame a beautiful vista of the scenic Oregon coastline. In the middle distance is Haystack Rock and The Needles at Cannon Beach.

(Page 16) MOUNT HOOD ... A setting of beautiful contrasts on Lolo Pass in the Mt. Hood National Forest of Oregon. New autumn snows on the mountain and vivid colors of vine maple foliage contrast spectacularly against the dark evergreen forest.

(Pages 18 & 19) OREGON COAST ... The old Pacific was in a tranquil mood and the springtime weather at its best when this photo was taken on the rugged Southern Oregon coast, between Brookings and Pistol River.

(Page 21) CASCADE WINTER ... A sparkling star shines atop a snow-mantled Christmas tree in the Oregon Cascade Range.

(Page 23) MT. JEFFERSON WILDERNESS ... Wilderness flowers are sprinkled across the green alpine meadows surrounding Russell Lake at the foot of Mt. Jefferson. Several lakes in the area lure fishermen and campers to this mountain paradise. It can be reached by trail only.

(Page 33) SILVER FALLS STATE PARK ... The gold of autumn tinted maple foliage in the shadowy gorge where the lower South Falls pours in a silvery curtain over a cliff in Silver Falls State Park just east of Salem. A dozen waterfalls of various sizes are encompassed in this beautiful state park.

(Page 35) WILLAMETTE RIVER ... The Willamette River winds its way out of the Cascade Range foothills. The stream eventually becomes Oregon's largest river and traverses the state's richest agricultural valley to its confluence with the mighty Columbia River.

(Pages 36 & 37) THREE SISTERS WILDERNESS ... The middle and north Sister peaks rise above little Tam Lake, one of several beautiful gems in the Three Sisters Wilderness area on the crest of Oregon's Cascade Range.

(Pages 40 & 41) MT. JEFFERSON ... Mt. Jefferson and an unnamed lake, high in the Cascade Range.

(Pages 44 & 45) TODD LAKE AND MOUNT BACHELOR ... Todd Lake nestles in lush green meadows and forests at the foot of Mt. Bachelor on the crest of the Oregon Cascade Range. Todd Lake is a popular camping area reached by a short forest road from the Cascade Lakes Highway. Mt. Bachelor is a year round recreation area. A lodge and ski-lifts lure winter sports enthusiasts and summer sightseers to the slopes of the mountain.

(Page 57) HECETA HEAD LIGHT ... The Heceta Head Light flashes its million candle-power warning across the Pacific surf from its perch on the rocky promontory of Heceta Head on the central Oregon coast.

(Page 64) OREGON COAST STORM ... Storm watching on the coast is a favorite adventure for Oregonians during the winter months, when more often than not, the Pacific surf stages a tempestuous show. This scene is at Yachats State Park with Cape Perpetua veiled by mists.

(Page 69) FAIRY FALLS ... Fairy Falls leaps over a cliff of lava in a forest of Oregon Cascade Range. It is reached by a two-mile trail climb from the Columbia River Highway.

(Page 72) OREGON FARMLAND ... Lush green grainfields and nut orchards contrast in a pleasing pattern with summer fallow in the picturesque Iowa Hills bordering the fertile Tualatin Valley of western Oregon.

11   (Left) McKENZIE RIVER . . . Oregon's famed McKenzie River flows swiftly down the forested slopes of the Cascade Range.

(Upper) GOODPASTURE BRIDGE . . . The Goodpasture covered bridge at Vida, Oregon, spanning the famed McKenzie River.

(Lower) MT. HOOD AT SUNRISE . . . Residents of various sections of Portland are treated to a spectacle of indescribable beauty as the rising sun silhouettes the lofty volcanic cone of Mt. Hood and the Cascade crest on the distant horizon. A sea of fog sometimes envelopes the city and the Willamette Valley, a thousand feet below.

17   (Upper) PORTLAND, OREGON . . . The famed International Rose Test Gardens in Portland, Oregon's Washington Park create a colorful foreground for a distant vista of Mt. Hood.
(Lower) LESLIE GULCH, OREGON . . . An improved road now provides access to spectacular scenic beauty of colorful stone spires and cliffs of Leslie Gulch in far eastern Oregon.

20   (Upper) EASTERN OREGON . . . Springtime runoff from the mountain over-flows from Burnt River near Harford, Oregon, creating lush grazing that will last far into the summer season for cattle.

(Lower) MT. THIELSON AND DIAMOND LAKE, OREGON . . . The precipitous volcanic spire of Mt. Thielson scrapes summertime clouds high above Diamond Lake in the Cascade Range of Oregon. This is without doubt the most popular fishing lake in the Pacific Northwest.

22   (Upper Left) CRATER LAKE . . . Summer snowfields cling to the steep walls of Crater Lake which rise nearly two thousand feet above the surface of the lake.
(Lower Left) ROGUE RIVER VALLEY . . . Winter snow lies deep on Mt. McLoughlin, on the horizon, despite the fact that spring has arrived in the Rogue River Valley's orchards and farmland.
(Upper Right) CRATER LAKE . . . A picturesque old snag still clings defiantly to rimrock a thousand feet above Crater Lake long after the tree has perished.
(Lower Right) ROGUE RIVER . . . A river boat in the hands of a skilled guide dashes through a boulder-strewn rapids of the famed Rogue River.

RHODODENDRON

CINQUEFOIL

LADY SLIPPER
TIGER LILY

INDIAN PAINT BRUSH

FOXGLOVE

SKUNK CABBAGE

Wild Flower Photo Descriptions

TIGER LILY ... A beautiful specimen of Tiger Lily in bloom beside a small tributary stream to the famed Rogue River in southern Oregon. Boating parties that make the river run from Grants Pass to Gold Beach are treated to intimate sights of wildlife and wild flowers enroute.

CINQUEFOIL . . . Cinquefoil bloom in golden beauty at the foot of a small waterfall in the Three Sisters Wilderness on the crest of the Cascade Range in Oregon. The clear waters of the stream reveal colorful volcanic stone over which it flows.

RHODODENDRON . . Wild rhododendron thrives in several regions of western Washington, western Oregon and northwestern California.

SKUNK CABBAGE . . . Because of its odor, skunk cabbage is an appropriate name for this colorful flowering plant that flourishes in swampy or damp areas of western Oregon and Washington. This swampy patch was photographed near the Oregon Coast.

LADY SLIPPER . . . A graceful cluster of Calypso, also known as Lady Slipper blossoms, a member of the Orchid family, flowering on the shadowed forest floor in the foothills of Oregon's Coast Range.

INDIAN PAINT BRUSH . . . An Indian Paint Brush glows in fluorescent beauty in an alpine meadow of Oregon's Cascade Range. The brilliant coloring is in the foliage rather than the blossom of this plant which creates a kaleidoscope of different shades in many areas of the Northwest.

FOXGLOVE . . . Wild Foxglove blooms in profusion in Western Oregon, Western Washington and Northwestern California. Digitalis is used in treatment of heart patients.

Northern Oregon

OREGON was originally the name for the Columbia, River of the West. This colossal waterway which divides Oregon and Washington is now held in check by four giant dams, yet it surges along with immense power along all 1,250 miles of its length from its source, Columbia Lake in Canada. When it finally crashes into the sea just past Astoria, its energy creates whirling cross-currents that send foaming water high into the air. The Columbia is a great showoff. It gets plenty of attention from native and out-of-state admirers who ride and hike along its banks. Long ago the lordly river cut a magnificent Gorge through the Cascades for itself, the better setting to receive the homage of its human subjects, who would arrive later upon the scene.

Portland, Oregon's flagship city, gains distinction from its position on the Columbia. Situated where the river turns north and is joined by the Willamette coming up from the south, the city is an important trading crossroads and possesses the West's largest fresh-water port. A feature that makes Portland truly an Oregon city is its extensive park system. Extending through sections of the downtown area are its unique "park blocks" — complete city blocks turned over entirely to open landscaped area. In addition to these blocks, on the western hills of the city is a 5,000-acres park system that extends for nine miles and where deer and smaller wild animals find a refuge.

Portland, with its flavor of lumber mills and its artifacts of the history of wood products manufacture, is only one of a string of towns along the Columbia that have been part of the Northwest story. Some of them, downstream of Portland, are now ghost towns: first Linnton, then farther westward along the river, Fort William, Mayger, Bradwood, and Clifton. Other, very much alive towns in this same stretch—like St. Helens, Scappoose, and Clatskanie—have in their midst relics of a past age, and if one drives U.S. 30 which connects them he is likely to come upon many bits of backcountry nostalgia. The Hudson's Bay Company, for example, contributed some of the residents of the Scappoose cemetery, and St. Helens' Courthouse Square is from another era. If one follows U.S. 30 all the way, he ends up, of course, at Astoria, Oregon's northernmost city, and as steeped in legend as any place in the West. Astoria watches over the last stretch of the Columbia, where the great river, now five miles wide, casts its stupendous volume of water into the Pacific.

East of Portland, history and legend combine to lend color to the Oregon towns along the river bank. Cascade Locks, near Bonneville, preserves the past and the legends in a splendid small museum. Where the lock walls now stand, a natural bridge once spanned the river, according to Indian legend. The bridge was cast into the river by Tyhee Sahale, the Supreme Being, angered by his two sons' feud over the beautiful guardian of the bridge's sacred flame. In typical mythological style, the debris created the river's cascades, and the three lovers, who came out second-best in the bridge-hurling spree, were resurrected as Mt. Hood, Mt. Adams, and Mt. St. Helens.

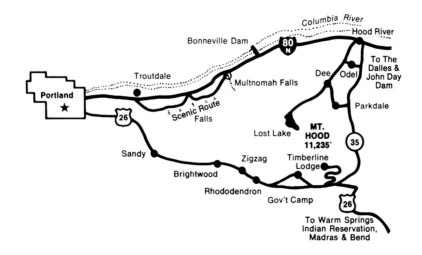

A trip east from Portland along the Columbia can be historic, as we have noted, but it is, above all, scenic. The "loop trip" from Portland is only some 170 miles and is a fine way to see both the spectacular river scenery and all of the faces of the equally magnificent Mt. Hood. The route takes highway 80N to Hood River, but for a heightened experience of the river and its forested banks, one should drive the old scenic highway for the 24 miles from Troutdale to a little east of Multnomah Falls. This road dictates a slower pace and comes into more intimate proximity with the many breathtaking waterfalls along the Gorge. The views of the Gorge itself are much more satisfying from the high perspective of this road.

At the end of the river segment is Hood River at the end of the Hood River Valley, famous for its varied and abundant crops of fruit. Highway 35 aims south from Hood River and starts the circuit of Mt. Hood. One side trip from this road is to Lost Lake, for an unsurpassed view of the peak. The highway follows the east fork of Hood River until it turns southwest to meet U.S. 26 coming up from the south. At this point a short sidetrip takes one to the famous Timberline Lodge, on the slopes of Mt. Hood. Timberline is of course a great skiing facility, but its attraction for tourists is year-round. Driving west back to Portland one goes through lush forests and quaint mountain towns, then farmland and gently rolling hills. It's a trip whose unique charms will remain long in one's memory.

Northern Oregon Coast

EARLY explorers such as Captain James Cook and Sir Francis Drake found the Oregon Coast a rugged and violent introduction to an all but empty land. Hundreds of years later much of the Coast is still a solitary place, fascinating and mysterious. Oregon meets the sea along a 400-mile shoreline, from Astoria at its northern limit to Brookings close to the California border. A relatively small percentage of people around the country are aware of the beauty and variety of Oregon's Coast. The residents seem to prefer it that way, for too many human intruders possibly could steal some of the magic away from "their" Coast with its long, lonely beaches and half-hidden crescent coves stacked with driftwood and beach rocks.

Perhaps nowhere else in the state is the restorative magic of Oregon so pervasive as it is on the Coast. What some of the affluent seek, spending fortunes around the world, is available free for anyone who has the good sense and insight to spend a day or longer just being a part of this land-sea ambiance. Peace of mind, tranquillity, renewal—call it what you will; a feeling of self-forgetfulness and calm is the reward for the solitary beachcomber, the explorer of tide pools, rocks, and lonely stands of coast pine and spruce.

U.S. Highway 101 skirts the shoreline for much of the way, and those who prefer quick glimpses and changes of mood will find a fascinating kaleidoscope of scenic variety as they drive along the winding road. The highway sometimes ventures a few miles farther inland, offering views of coastal flora such as rhododendron, azalea, and salal. Each town has its unique qualities, readily revealed by the residents to visitors who show an interest. The northern coastline contains the more developed or "commercial" stretches, such as those at Seaside, Cannon Beach, Lincoln City, Depoe Bay, and Newport. But even these coastal spots are not crowded affairs in the "Coney Island" sense. Even in midsummer one can stake a claim to a large stretch of unoccupied beach or go sightseeing along the bays and boat basins without stepping on the heels of other people doing the same thing.

For the person who feels he must "do" something wherever he goes, towns on the northern coast offer many activities. At Astoria, fishing is a big attraction and history is a long suit. The visitor can explore the city's past in a museum or watch, from the hilly site of the Astor Column, giant freighters heading up the Columbia or gliding seaward under the four-mile-long Astoria Bridge. Seaside, south of Astoria, has a fine swimming beach in the manner of some of the New Jersey ocean resorts, and Oregon's version of a carnival atmosphere. Cannon Beach also has a popular bathing beach, with Haystack Rock standing a little out to sea; there's also an artists' colony where one can browse and discover interesting uses for driftwood and rock treasures picked up while beachcombing. Lincoln City, farther down the Coast, is very visitor-oriented and has been integrated with a string of smaller communities into what is called, in the chamber-of-commerce idiom, the "20 Miracle Miles." Depoe Bay has a thriving charter business for those who like deep-sea fishing and a spectacular scenic loop road for an impressive perspective of the Pacific. At Newport, although many activities beckon the visitor, the pace is slow and inviting, especially on the Yaquina Bay waterfront where the fishermen gather.

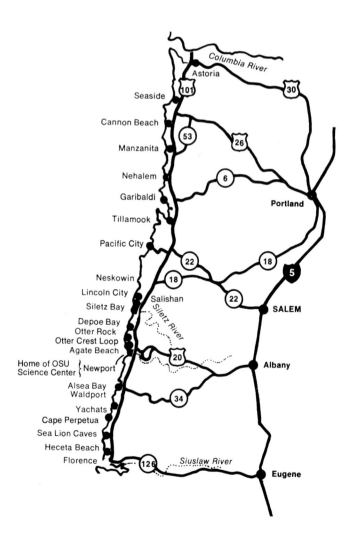

Moving down the coast past the charming villages of Waldport and Yachats, the highway climbs high on the shoulders of Cape Perpetua, a massive and lofty rock cliff rising abruptly out of the sea. From the top of the Cape, where a side road leads, the view to the north and south is one of the best in the whole stretch of shoreline. Cape Perpetua also has a Visitor Center with trails leading from it through the tide pool and plant areas of the Cape, where visitors may stroll, study the marine and plant life, and learn about the geological history of the area.

Heceta Head and its lighthouse, next prominent feature of the Cape area, is one of the most photographed places on the Coast. It and the Devil's Churn are but a short distance from Sea Lion Caves, where the visitor can stand on a windy cliff and watch thousands of sea lions taking the sun far below, or he can descend into the interior of the Caves via elevator for an intimate look at the interior of the cavern that serves the wild sea lions as a year-round home. Mention of sea lions brings to mind the growing population of sea otters all along the Coast. The growing numbers of these creatures, once nearly exterminated, testify to the effectiveness of Oregon's measures to protect endangered species.

Florence, at about the mid-point on the Coast, is another town that welcomes the visitor but doesn't smother him with this-to-buy and that-to-do. It has an old town section worth exploring, and its South Jetty Road meanders along flat and wide stretches of beach, nearly deserted except when the hottest days of summer bring the parched valley population to where the cool ribbons of sand and beach grass glisten invitingly as the cool Pacific tide rolls over them.

Southern Oregon Coast

THOSE strange, sandy phenomena of nature, the Oregon Dunes, begin just south of Florence and are certainly the dominant feature of the southern half of the Coast for the 45 miles that they stretch toward Coos Bay. The dunes are usually enormous, rolling and rising to heights of more than 250 feet. One would logically conclude that masses of sand of such girth would also be quite substantial, but their contours are continually changing, with the wind acting as a tireless sculptor. A huge dune seen one week may be a deep sand canyon the next, or appear to have lent its mass to a neighboring monster. The Oregon Dunes National Recreation Area marks out the most stupendous works of the windy carver in sand. This is part of Oregon's Coast that lays valid claim to the term, "unique." And if the visitor is not content just to be in the midst of this undulating "Sahara by the Sea" (so-called in a State Highway Department travel promotion), he can ride the stark, roller-coaster landscape in a dune buggy.

Along with the giant sand dunes, this coastal stretch is lavishly endowed with forests and fresh-water lakes and streams, so that in some places one may actually dip one foot in the salty ocean while letting the cool fresh water of a rivulet course between the toes of his other foot. Honeyman State Park, three miles below Florence has this kind of variety within its borders. The park's environments of lake, woods, and dunes get along very well together. Some 16 more lakes between Florence and North Bend are favorite fishing and camping spots. Some of the names—Cleawox, Woahink, Siltcoos, and Tahkenitch—have links to Indian tribal cultures of the past.

Reedsport, another pleasant coast town, is about halfway between Florence and Coos Bay. It is the western terminus of the Umpqua, one of Oregon's more placid rivers, at least along its lower stretches. The Umpqua rises in the Cascades and pursues a meandering course west and northwest through the Coast Range. If one follows it from the valley town of Drain along an easy, broad road to the Coast, he can partake of no more sumptuous riverine beauty anywhere. Coos Bay, a little way down the line (with its partner city, North Bend), is the premier lumber shipping port of the world. It can also be boastful about its striped bass fishing. South of this town are four of the 32 coastal state parks along the long coastline. The four parks—Sunset Beach, Shore Acres, Cape Arago, and Bullards Beach—are in settings of extraordinary beauty. Nearly all of Oregon's coast,

by the way, is in public ownership, another example of the progressive spirit that has long been associated with the people of this state.

This stretch begins the wildest and loneliest part of the coastline. One can drive the 40-odd miles from Coos Bay to Cape Blanco and Port Orford with little for company except sea, sand, sky, and the highway. There are some towns along the way, but they are only minor interruptions in the general solitude of the seascape and landscape. Cape Blanco is the westernmost point in Oregon. It has a picturesque lighthouse, and its setting is another example of the magnificence that is characteristic of the Coast. Port Orford was founded by a redoubtable sea captain and his crew, whose skirmishes with the local Indians are remembered at Battle Rock Wayside, south of town.

The southern Coast has its own private and separate peak—Humbug Mountain, six miles below Battle Rock. This 1750-foot-high eminence is also a state park and

a beach. Here the persevering beachcomber may find all sorts of riches yielded by the sea; treasures such as Japanese glass floats, bottles, marine fossils, jasper, petrified wood, bamboo, kegs, and driftwood. If he is really fortunate the beach visitor may look out to sea just when a school of whales is passing, or second best, some sea lions and sea otters.

Pushing on the 28 miles to Gold Beach, one is getting close to the California border. Gold Beach has become known as the place to make those 32-mile trips up the untamed Rogue River to Agness. Mail boats daily leave the Wedderburn dock just north of Gold Beach for the 64-mile round-trip, taking on tourists for the thrilling run by jet-powered boat. South of Gold Beach the scenery is just as showy, and before arriving at Brookings on the border, the traveler may be moved to gape at the colossal rock formations rising from the sea, at the wild flowers growing from dunes, or at the sweeping undulations of the coastal countryside. The piece de résistance is at Brookings, where Azalea State Park, named for its sprawling acres of azaleas, offers an idyllic setting for a rest and a meal, with wild cherries, violets, butterflies, and hummingbirds for company.

If one has (heaven forbid!) traveled the whole Oregon Coast in a day or two, his impressions will most assuredly be a kind of patchwork. He will have passed by the riches around him too fast for true appreciation, and he will have missed the whole point of this part of the Oregon experience. For the renewal that is offered to the Oregon traveler is a fragile gift that must be accepted on its own terms. To receive it requires a standstill attitude of mind and a willingness to pause and consider one's place in all this beauty.

Willamette Valley

PICTURE one of the richest agricultural areas anywhere, a broad swath of land that stretches eastward to the high Cascades and west to the Coast Range. At the north end is Portland and at the south, Eugene. In this fertile valley known as the Willamette, lives the major part of Oregon's population. The Willamette River, on or near whose banks much of the state's history was made, winds through the valley from south to north. In former days the river was used as the only means of transportation, until the railroads took over that task in the 1870s.

The three biggest Oregon cities—including Salem and the two above, Eugene and Portland—are situated along the river. But a smaller town than these can claim more historical glory. This is Oregon City, just south of Portland. It was the first incorporated town west of the Mississippi and the territorial seat of government before Oregon became a state. Oregon City is a rather retiring sort of town, so few people—even Oregonians—are fully appreciative of its historical importance. The city's founder, Dr. John McLoughlin, figured prominently in the western operations of the Hudson's Bay Company. Today his house is a national historic site. There are also other buildings which are reminders of Oregon City's — and Oregon's — past, and two historic burial grounds.

South from Oregon City, near the geographical center of the Willamette Valley, is Salem, the capital. Theodore Winthrop, the mid-nineteenth-century traveler in the Northwest, described Salem as "a village on one of those exquisite plains . . . where the original oak trees have been left about." Many of the murals and sculpture of the State Capitol are based on themes concerned with the Lewis and Clark expeditions. Salem is a calm, quiet place for a city of its size and importance. One of the important things it does every year is play host to the Oregon State Fair in late summer, when the myriad products of the fertile Willamette farmland are symbolized in carefully arranged exhibits. The Willamette River in the general Salem area has a special picturesque side in three backcountry free ferries: one near Canby, the Wheatland ferry between Newberg and Salem, and the Buena Vista ferry northwest of Albany. All three ferry crossings have strong links to the nineteenth century in Oregon.

About 50 miles east of Salem is Detroit Dam, one of man's more successful manipulations of raw nature. The dam backs up the North Santiam River for eight and a half miles, creating Detroit Lake, and an out-of-charac-

ter tranquility for the normally impetuous river that flashes down from the Mt. Jefferson Wilderness. The narrow canyon where the dam restrains the river has a fairyland quality about it. Standing on the ramparts of the dam, one sees in one direction the lovely blue lake reflecting, jewel-like, the perfection of its setting; on the other side, looking down as from the prow of a ship, one can see far below on the canyon floor the leaping, dancing river rejoicing in being free once more of constraints. The mists sent up the canyon walls by the churning water add to the dream-like feeling.

At the southern terminus of the Willamette Valley, Eugene sits astride the river like some very authoritative matron intent on meeting all travelers before they are allowed to pass on their way. The image may be a little strained, but here where the mountains start to pinch off the valley, one is almost driven into the arms of this lumbering capital of 90,000. But that's not so bad. Eugene is a friendly place. Add to this the hard-to-find mixture of rural beauty and metropolitan sophistication, and a picture of an attractive community emerges.

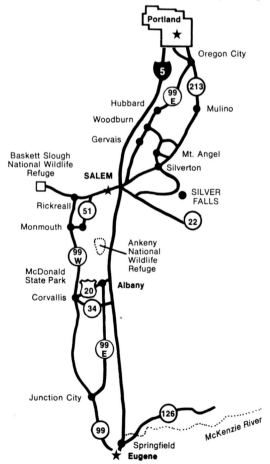

34 (Upper) STEENS MOUNTAIN . . . The snow-flecked Steens Mountain rises sharply several thousand feet above eastern Oregon desert land, once again illustrating the many contrasts of the state of Oregon, generally better known for its dense forests and abundant rainfall.

(Lower) OWYHEE RIVER . . . Cliffs and buttes rise steeply above the Owyhee River in eastern Oregon. This comparatively arid land of sage brush and rocks is quite a change from the green forests and lush vegetation of western Oregon.

38   (Upper) SPARKS LAKE . . . A doe and two fawn wander along a picturesque island in Sparks Lake at the foot of the South Sister, one of the high volcanic peaks on the crest of the Central Cascade Range of Oregon.

(Lower) OREGON FOREST . . . Wherever there is an open glade where sunlight can reach the floor of the Northwest's forests, vine maple foliage is transformed with brilliant autumn coloring.

(Right) THREE SISTERS WILDERNESS . . . The South Sister, towering above Green Lakes, is framed by evergreen trees in the Three Sisters Wilderness Area. This beautiful group of lakes nestles in a valley between high peaks of the Cascade Range. The area can be visited only by trail.

42 (Upper) THREE SISTERS WILDERNESS . . . Brilliantly colored Indian Paint Brush photographed beside a clear mountain stream in an alpine meadow on the crest of Oregon's Cascade Range.

(Lower) THE SOUTH SISTER . . . One of Oregon's loftiest volcanic peaks scrapes the clouds above one of the Green Lakes in the Three Sisters Wilderness Area. This beautiful region in the Central Cascade Range of Oregon is penetrated by trail only.

47

(Left) THE THREE SISTERS WILDERNESS AREA . . . Brokentop Mountain rises high above Park Meadows, where a clear stream flows through the meadows. This area can be reached by a short hike.

(Right) SPARKS LAKE . . . Islands of trees thrust through the mirror-like waters of Sparks Lake, reflecting the volcanic cone of Brokentop Mountain in the central Cascade Range of Oregon.

(Lower) EAGLE CREEK TRAIL . . . The popular well-worn Eagle Creek trail reveals a wide variety of natural beauty, including the deciduous trees and shrubs on the floor of the forest along with giant evergreens.

48   (Upper) ROGUE RIVER . . . The Rogue River, world-famous fisherman's paradise in southern Oregon, is shown meandering leisurely seaward in a scene that is a great contrast to much of the river's turbulent course.

(Lower) SUNSET . . . Mt. McLoughlin and a flight of geese are silhouetted by a colorful sunset photographed across Klamath Lake, near the Klamath Wildlife Refuge.

Willamette Valley to Rogue River Country

FROM Eugene south to Grants Pass, about 138 miles, the terrain offers great variety, including wooded mountainsides, flashing rivers, and isolated valleys. It's a colorful historical area as well. Throughout the Bohemia Mining District southeast of Cottage Grove are reminders of gold mining, including the Bohemia Gold Mining Days celebration in July. Many of the mines are still in existence and may be visited by private car or in organized tours. The District is named for "Bohemia" Johnson who discovered gold in 1863 while he was supposedly hiding out in the Calapooya Mountains. Before long a hundred claims were staked out and the Bohemia Mining District was created. Other metals in addition to gold were found, but no great riches were dug out of the Bohemia. Now the charm of this part of Oregon is in the mining relics, the incredibly long views from the mountains round about, the wildlife, the racing mountain streams, and the dark gorges with their sharply sloping walls.

Just south of Cottage Grove, if one is driving along the north-south freeway, he has a chance to do some pleasant, easy exploring by car. At this point Highway 99 leaves the big Interstate 5 and takes off through the small lumbering towns of Drain, Yoncalla, Oakland, Sutherlin, Wilbur, Winchester, Winston, Dillard, and Myrtle Creek. Roseburg is in their midst, but since it is a "big" town, it is served by the freeway. From Roseburg one may visit the fascinating little country town of Lookingglass 10 miles west, where the only parking meter is in front of the general store.

The town of Drain is a key to Highway 38, which heads for the sea along the graceful lower Umpqua River, a stretch of waterway mentioned elsewhere in this book. But that isn't the whole story of the Umpqua. The lower Umpqua that meanders to the Pacific is but a short segment of the whole squiggly thread of river that finds its way through the hills north of Roseburg, after a journey from the high Cascades, as the North Umpqua River. The North Umpqua is paralleled faithfully by Oregon Highway 138, but drivers usually miss the best parts of a trip like this. It would be nice to have a pair of snap-on helicopter wings when mosying along the North Umpqua valley, because this is country meant for hovering and looking. The river shows many faces along this part of its length, and its moods range from calm through wild to savage. There are some odd rock chimneys and natural arches to stare at when you reach Dry Creek, 10 miles east of the town of Steamboat, as well as an Indian cave with pictographs on the walls.

Roseburg to Grants pass is full of great scenery, but a lot of it is found around communities which are reached only by side trips from the main highway. In Wolfcreek there's a big slice of history, as well. Wolfcreek Tavern is supposed to have sheltered, for a time, U. S. Grant when he was a second lieutenant touring the West. Other notables believed to have partaken of the inn's hospitality are General Sherman, Joaquin Miller, and even Jack London. Wolfcreek Road, starting near the tavern, is an adventurous way to get to Grants Pass. It brushes by old gold mines, backcountry settlements, and the glamorous Rogue River itself. At Grants Pass, the visitor has the opportunity to take full advantage of the Rogue. Guides take boats on long float trips to the Pacific lasting three or four days, or on short powered cruises up the river. Grants Pass is the northern gateway for Oregon Caves National Monument, tucked away in its spectacular setting high in the Siskiyous near the California border.

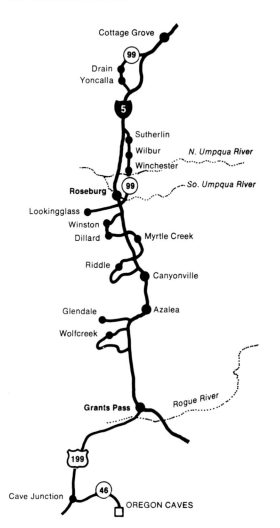

Central Oregon

CENTRAL Oregon is a kind of buffer between the lush vegetation and thick forests of the western slopes and the arid, open desert vistas of Eastern Oregon. It partakes of attributes of both regions and, in its own way, merits superlatives as extravagant as those used to portray the other areas. For the summer tourist, it fulfills all the extravagant descriptions that travel agents are wont to endow places with—"outdoor paradise," "crystal clear lakes abundant with trout," "magnificent scenic vistas." The city of Bend is generally considered the hub of the region. It is located at the middle of the north-south line. And it is the natural starting point for excursions into high mountains and ski slopes, for sorties into forests of jackpine and stands of Ponderosa, or rambles along the high valley floor where random growths of sage punctuate the open rangeland, reminding the traveler that to the east is a harsher clime and a thirstier land.

Bend, on the Deschutes River, is famous as a clean-looking, attractive resort and year-round-living town. Its sparkling looks, unbelievably clear, dry air (its elevation is 3,600 feet), and moderate climate make it a comfortable place to settle in. Century Drive, a well-known scenic route, begins and ends at Bend. Formally called Cascade Lakes Highway, the route forms a rough square, one segment of which soars 3,000 feet from Bend up into the heart of the Cascades. Along its 100-mile length, when not flirting with Bachelor Butte and some of the other handsome spires of the central Cascades, the road slices through Deschutes National Forest, rides over black lava flows, and passes cinder cones and obsidian cliffs. It crosses mountain meadows full of sweet-smelling wildflowers and touches near Forest Service campgrounds, primitive areas, and lakes, one of which —Elk—is a starting point for pack trains into the Three Sisters Wilderness. Hardly a sign of civilization disturbs the natural serenity of the scene until the road finally curves back to U.S. 97 for the final leg back to Bend. This part of the road touches turnoffs to lakes, craters, a lava forest, resort and recreation areas, a volcanic site, and lava and ice caves.

The scenic variety compressed into the comparatively few miles of Century Drive would make Central Oregon sufficient unto itself if that was the whole story. But anyone who has been north to Redmond, Prineville, Madras, and the Warm Springs Reservation with its Indian-operated resort, Kah-Nee-Ta, would be loath to leave out these contributors to the area's attractions. Prineville, 15 miles east of Redmond, leads into the

beautiful Ochoco mountains. Nearby are the Ochoco and Prineville reservoirs, and east of the mountains is a small but fascinating area called the Painted Hills, whose barren landscape of treeless mounds and gullies is thought to have been created in the distant past by volcanic activity in the Cascades. The striated coloration of the hills increases the eerie unreality of the place.

A few miles north of Redmond the north-south highway (U.S. 97) passes over the Crooked River Gorge, a deep, sheer-sided canyon carved by the river, still carving far below in the canyon floor as it twists on its serpentine course. To the north on the same road is Madras, an agricultural center. Northwest of Madras is

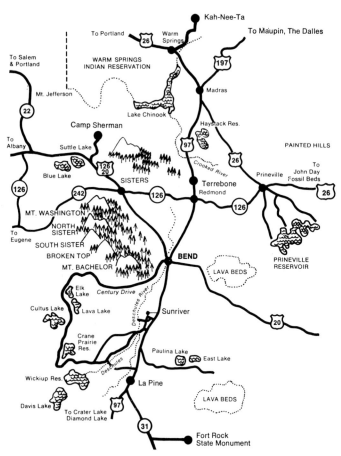

the Warm Springs Reservation and the elegant spa, Kah-Nee-Ta. This region of high plateaus, giant natural sculptures, and awesome coloring stirs memories of many a story of the Old West and the harsh lives endured by the early inhabitants.

One of the ever-present rewards of travel in central Oregon is the view to the west. There, seemingly close at hand, the Cascades rise in beauty sharply chiseled by the clear atmosphere. The peaks burst suddenly from the valley floor in an awesome show of strength and majesty, and the whole range stretches like a mighty wall, fading in the blue, purple, and yellow haze to the north and south.

The Mountains

OREGON'S Cascade Range dominates the state's mountain environment, because, with their height and unbroken line from north to south, they are a major regulating factor in the state's weather. And their timbered wealth gives them first place in Oregon's economy. The Cascades are almost-extinct volcanoes. The "almost" lends excitement to their character. Volcanism is said to have begun in the Cascades about 10 million years ago and is still slowing to a stop. Although they are not likely to erupt, Hood, Rainier, and some other Cascade peaks have vents from which steam issues.

The dramatic beauty of the Cascade peaks is nowhere more apparent than in the Central Cascades. Here the Mt. Jefferson Wilderness Area sets off the rugged, snowy peak that rises more than 10,000 feet. Jefferson Park below the mountain is a favorite spot for hikers and nature lovers because of its alpine meadows, its wildflowers, and its streams and lakes. Farther south, about 70 miles due east of Eugene, are the Three Sisters—North, Middle, and South—all over 10,000 feet. They also have their own wilderness area, but hiking to them is not necessary to get a "close-up" look. The McKenzie Pass from Eugene provides motorists a spectacular view at close range of these beauties, as well as sights of other peaks far away to the north and south. The Pass itself takes second place to none of the Cascades' scenic delights. For some 50 miles it parallels the McKenzie River, one of the most glamorous recreational streams in the West. Then in the area of its summit, the Pass shows off a jumble of black lava, one of the most impressive flows in the United States.

South of the Three Sisters, and reached by side roads off Highway 58 from Eugene, is a group of high mountain lakes and reservoirs of great beauty. One of these is Waldo Lake, the second largest natural lake in Oregon. The U.S. Forest Service has taken great pains to preserve the beautiful alpine aspect of this lake. Some of the other lakes in this mountain area, the first two of which are accessible from Highway 58, are Odell, Crescent, Davis, and Cultus.

To the north and south of the Central Cascades are a number of mountain landmarks of distinctive grandeur, the most notable and obvious being Mt. Hood, the monarch of Oregon mountains. Hood is a much-climbed and visited mountain and a popular skiing area on its lower reaches. But its proximity to Portland and accessibility via trails and settlements on its approaches do not diminish its hypnotic fascination for anyone who gazes at it. Hood is visible from almost any high point in the state, but one of the most magical views of the mountain is from the western hills of Portland, where it seems to float lightly just above the eastern skyline. Man has paid tribute to this magic mountain by building on its flank a ski lodge of gargantuan proportions and ornate art—Timberline Lodge. The Lodge was completed in 1937 as a project of the Works Progress Administration and stands as the expression of the work of many artisans.

The southern Cascades have their fair share of impressive and towering peaks: Diamond Peak, Mt. Scott, Mt. Thielsen, Mt. McLoughlin. And there are a few areas reserved for wilderness. West and south of Odell Lake is the Diamond Peak Wilderness, easily accessible, like the Three Sisters Wilderness to the north. In contrast to this is the Mountain Lakes Wilderness northwest of Klamath Falls. This relatively unknown area is part of the Winema National Forest. Because most of the Wilderness is above the 6,000-foot level, trails are often blocked until late June by heavy snows.

Southern Oregon

THE loose regional label, "Southern Oregon," is hard-pressed to cover all of the vast area that makes up the southern part of the state. Part of the problem is in the way Oregonians think about their state. In the west, the Umpqua and Rogue valleys are considered as very much separate from the Southern Oregon that forms the Crater Lake and Klamath Falls areas to the east, and certainly not in the least identifiable with southeastern Oregon. The narrow valleys of the southern Cascades and Siskiyous are more "west" than south, having greater affinities with the Willamette Valley to the north than with any other area.

The western portion of southern Oregon is a region whose topography and climate mark it as a transitional area between the damp west and drier east. It is a combination of dry chaparral, gold and green rolling hills, and green forests similar to the thick fir stands characteristic of more northerly parts of the state. The biggest town in this varied region is Medford, center of a lush orchard country whose plentiful water, fertile lands, and long, warm summers produce pears, peaches, and other fruit of a quality unsurpassed anywhere. Medford is also the center of a thriving resort area, drawing large numbers of retired persons, who are attracted by its dry air, lakes, many fishing streams, and natural beauty.

Just a few miles west of Medford is Jacksonville, which still projects the excitement of the gold-rush days. The old county courthouse is now a museum, and many of the buildings and homes, with their turrets, gables, and intricate woodwork, have been preserved to maintain their nineteenth-century character. In August the Peter Britt Music Festival is held here.

Ashland, south of Medford, is a contrast to the mining towns of the Rogue area. For many years it has been known before all else as the home of the celebrated Oregon Shakespearean Festival, launched in 1935 by Angus Bowmer, a member of the Southern Oregon College faculty. Performances are given in beautiful Lithia Park, designed by John McLaren, the creator of San Francisco's Golden Gate Park. Mt. Ashland, 7,523 feet high, dominates this exquisite setting, with its outdoor and indoor theatres, placed alongside a little jewel of a lake in the park. That leaves us to consider the south-central and southeastern regions, from Klamath Falls east to the border.

About 60 miles north of Klamath Falls lies one of the most glamorous and mystical ornaments in the Cascade diadem. Crater Lake, whose indescribable beauty has evoked more description than any other single geo-logical feature of Oregon, still defies the limited power of words to convey the full range of its magic. One of nature's colossal rearrangements of her decor, Crater Lake was formed from the explosion and collapse of Mt. Mazama, when the shell of the volcano gradually filled with rain. The lake is the deepest on the continent (more than 2,000 feet), about 20 square miles in area, and with two islands whose names, Wizard and Phantom Ship, tell much about the effect of the area on those who visit it.

Within a short range of Klamath Falls are many and varied natural attractions. Lake of the Woods, about 30 miles away, is guarded by 9,495-foot Mt. McLoughlin. And Upper Klamath National Wildlife Refuge, a sanctuary for waterfowl, is even closer. Collier Memorial State Park, 30 miles north, contains logging equipment used in earlier times and reconstructed loggers' shacks. Within the park, Spring Creek and Williamson River make their contributions to the idyllic scenery, and the nearby Sprague River beckons sports fishermen. Chiloquin, three miles south, displays Indian regional history

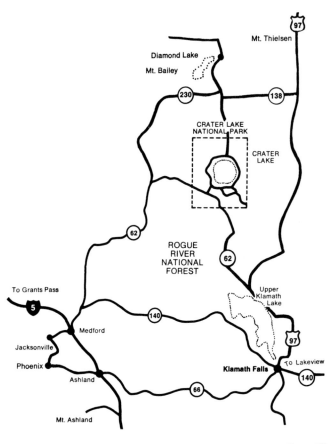

Southern Oregon

in its Klamath Indian Memorial Museum. Not to neglect the obvious, huge Upper Klamath Lake is never very far away. Klamath Falls is at the southern tip, and roads skirt the east and west shores of the stretched-out lake. Some of the area's pelicans stay at Lake Ewauna in downtown Klamath Falls, apparently preferring a taste of city life. To the south and east of Klamath Falls, the villages of Merrill, Malin, and Bonanza are picturesque examples of Oregon's rural communities.

History is part of the daily life of Klamath Falls. There are buildings still in use, like the Baldwin Hotel, which have physical evidence of their relationship with the past. Several museums containing artifacts of western history and art, give our emotional link with history a constant infusion of strength.

A long hop to the east, almost 100 miles by road, is Lakeview, almost in the middle of southern Oregon, and the highest, at 4,800 feet, of any town in the state. Although it is still a marketing town for large cattle spreads in the area, the days of great herds and round-ups are over, and Lakeview has become a headquarters for tourist forays into the region's desert country, unspoiled lakes, and other scenic attractions. One of these attractions, just beyond the edge of town, is "Old Perpetual," the only continuously spouting geyser in the United States, shooting its steaming column of water 60 feet into the air. Fifteen miles south, there's Goose Lake, which extends halfway into California. To the west, beyond Quartz Mountain Pass, the Gearhart Mountain Wilderness is a refuge for large animal populations.

About 20 miles north of Lakeview Abert Lake mirrors the desert alongside U.S. 395. On the eastern lake edge Abert Rim, a giant fault scarp, pushes with a startling abruptness 2,000 feet above the pleateau. From the summit of this sheer precipice the shimmering vision of desolate plains and hills is an indelible experience.

Still farther north, on Oregon 31, are Paisley, a former cattle town, and Summer Lake, whose waters are strongly alkaline and, in some years, scarce. As Oregon 31 continues on north and west it passes the wide plains and low hills of Fort Rock Valley, whose caves have revealed much evidence of the human hunting and fishing cultures 10,000 and more years ago.

Northeast of Lakeview is the magnificent and unique Hart Mountain National Antelope Refuge. Antelope, mule deer, bighorn sheep, and many other species are protected on this volcanic massif which reaches 3,000 feet above the plain. The Refuge area is a complete ecological universe. Its zones range from hot semidesert to snowy mountain, and the Warner Lakes grouping to the west is home for hundreds of thousands of birds. The explorer of the Hart Mountain area will find rough roads and few comforts, but much unspoiled landscape.

When one traces with his finger on a map of southeastern Oregon, he can find scant evidence of man's incursions. Oregon Highway 140 takes off east from a few miles north of Lakeview, and it passes only one village in Oregon before dipping down into Nevada on its 102-mile journey to Denio. What remain to the east are the Steens Mountains, U.S. Highway 95 slashing north-south through the mountains and prairies, the upper Owyhee River and its canyon, and a lot of empty land in between. Near the border, but more northerly than Lakeview's latitude, the Owyhee hills spread out in the sun to the north of Jordan Valley on the eastern border. This is Oregon's Basque country, or former Basque country, for even this mostly man-forsaken area has been Americanized and homogenized. The Basque herders with their thousands of sheep covering the Owyhee hills are gone. The original Basques from the Pyrenees are retired, have passed on, or are doing other things. Their music and speech, once predominant in Jordan Valley, are rarely heard, although the old-timers sometimes get together to speak the mother tongue.

One constant of this region has been its isolation from the rest of Oregon. Jordan Valley, whose population is now about 200, is farther from the nearest sizable settlement than any other Oregon town. It is still a very colorful place all through its rather limited extent. Some of its buildings are eloquent witnesses to the early part of this century. Built of native stone, they include a church, a hotel (abandoned), and a general store with a wooden sidewalk.

West of the Steens, back across the barren land, is the town of Frenchglen. Its population of 20 or so makes it a good-sized settlement for this part of Oregon. The town's strongly frontier-style hotel is worth a long look. Its rough-hewn lobby serves as a gathering place in the evenings for the few human beings around.

Eastern Oregon

SOMETIMES a regional label isn't tailored to make the perfect umbrella for a whole area. Here and there some of the landscape oozes into territory that people have classified, for their convenience, as something else. Eastern Oregon is like this. Its natural western border might be considered the Deschutes River which flows from below Bend north to the Columbia, but the Central Oregon people claim identification with a lot of that area. Its southern stretches blend into the desolate reaches of southeastern Oregon. No matter if they're a little hazy around the edges, the eastern lands have a flavor that's distinctive enough to give the visitor a sense of where he is.

Some people think they're in Eastern Oregon at The Dalles. It's a good starting point because of its place in history, for here is where the Oregon Trail finally jumped the Cascades (in 1845). The trail cut over the mountains to Oregon City was named the Barlow Road, in honor of the man who made it possible.

Some of the "real" east of Oregon is the country around Pendleton, still in the north but 130 miles deeper into the east. Pendleton is the largest town in Eastern Oregon and of course is home of the famous Roundup, held every September. Rodeo cowboys come from all over the country to compete, and many tribes are represented by hundreds of Indian performers. Just east of Pendleton is the Umatilla Indian Reservation, where the reservation road follows the old Oregon Trail for several miles. A little farther on is Bingham Springs, on the edge of the Blue Mountains, and the freeway (80N) follows the Oregon Trail southeast over the Blue Mountains to La Grande.

La Grande and its environs are worth a long pause. To the north lies the perfectly flat Grande Ronde Valley, a fascinating panorama of lush farms that can be seen in one sweep of the eye from vantage points on nearby heights. The past and present are next-door neighbors here: North Powder, to the south, reminds one of the stagecoach era; 20 miles to the west is Anthony Lakes, a sparkling recreation area perched 7,000 feet up in the Blue Mountains' Elkhorn Range. Imbler, a few miles north of La Grande, possesses some reminders of the late nineteenth century. The town of Cove to the east sits on the edge of the Grande Ronde Valley, where the Wallowas proclaim their dominion. Cove and Union, to the south, have some buildings from the Victorian era.

The configurations of the Wallowas remind the visitor of Alpine settings — the region is often called the "Switzerland of America." The wilderness at the heart of the Wallowas goes by the name "Wallowa Wonderland." Wallowa Lake, the largest of 60 lakes in these mountains, is south of the "cow town" of Joseph close to the eastern border. The lake reflects the snow-covered Wallowa peaks, some of which tower more than 10,000 feet over it. The tallest and most impressive are Sacajawea Peak and the Matterhorn, a near replica of the other Matterhorn. Pack trains are available for exploring the Eagle Cap Wilderness of the Wallowas. Or, the visitor may ride the recently built aerial tramway that soars up from the 4,000-foot level of the nearby lake to the top of 8,000-foot Mt. Howard. To the east and south is the historic town of Oxbow, then Oxbow Dam, holding back the savage Snake River, with the help of Hell's Canyon to the north and Brownlee to the south. One of the best places to gaze down into Hell's Canyon, the deepest gorge on the continent, is at Hat Point, 56 miles from Joseph. At an altitude of 6,982 feet, Hat Point looks down 5,700 feet to the Snake.

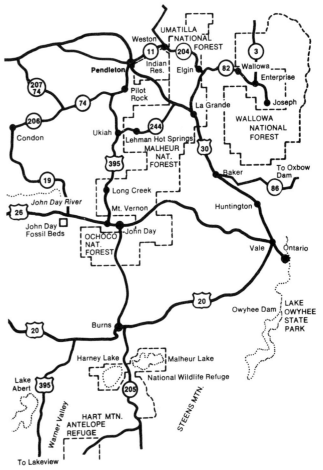

Eastern Oregon

Bending around to the west, the traveler comes to Baker, once the center of Oregon's gold country. The mining camps lived only briefly, leaving a few tumble-down cabins as testimony to their existence. Sumpter, 26 miles west, was the largest of the mining towns. It had 3,000 residents in the 1890s. Now it has about 150. The scenery in this valley is superb, even if the gold mines were not. But the ghost towns that were once centers of mining activity are now lending their picturesque remains to the decor around Baker.

The John Day country to the west, sandwiched within the Malheur National Forest, has its particular sense of history. The famous fossil beds in this region record geological history of millions of years, dating back to the time when most of Oregon was covered by the sea. John Day itself is a legendary cattle town where, up to a few years ago, massive cattle drives were conducted down Main Street. The proximity of the Strawberry Range of the Blue Mountains and the bright meadowland around the town give it an appearance of rugged beauty. Another reminder of the wild west era in this part of Oregon is nearby Canyon City, rich with history of the gold rush days. Canyon City is also the home of Joaquin Miller, the "Poet of the Sierra," whose cabin is on the grounds of a historical museum. In its heyday, Canyon City had a population of more than 10,000. Now it has about 700 inhabitants. Burns, some 70 miles due south of John Day, was once the center of a great cattle empire, and more great names in cattle ranching are associated with it than with any other place in Oregon.

58 (Upper) CAPE KIWANDA . . . A Pacific breaker explodes against an offshore rock to hurl a fountain of water high above the surf at picturesque Cape Kiwanda on the Oregon Coast.

(Lower) HONEYMAN STATE PARK . . . Cleawox Lake in Honeyman State Park mirrors early morning light on sand dunes that extend for more than a mile to the sea from this beautiful fresh water lake. Honeyman State Park also has outstanding campgrounds, picnic facilities and woodland trails, as well as boating and fishing on Woahink Lake, much larger than Cleawox Lake.

(Right) THE OREGON COAST . . . Flowering foxglove and wild iris mingle their color with huckleberry foliage and evergreens in Boardman State Park overlooking the Pacific Ocean in southwest Oregon.

61 (Left) SUNSET ... A picturesque wind-blown tree in Sam Boardman State Park on the southern Oregon coast is silhouetted by a colorful sunset.

(Lower) OREGON COAST SAND DUNES ... Prevailing coastal winds keep the vast area of sand dunes on the move. Here, the edge of an evergreen forest has become engulfed by the shifting dunes.

(Upper Left) SMELT RUN ... There's lots of fun and excitement when the smelt run is on at Yachats on the central Oregon coast. The 'pepper and salt' coarse-grained volcanic sand of Yachats beach is one of the few areas on the northwest coast where the smelt choose to lay their eggs.

(Upper Right) OREGON SURF ... The Pacific surf churns against offshore rocks and cliffs on the rugged Oregon coast at Boardman Park.

62   (Upper) CAPE KIWANDA ... A Pacific breaker dances shoreward to the colorful sandstone cliffs of Cape Kiwanda on the Oregon Coast.
(Lower) OREGON COAST ... Surf fishing is good if the excitement of gulls is an indication, and it usually is.
(Right) OREGON COASTLINE ... A spectacular panorama of surf, shoreline and the Oregon coast highway viewed from Cape Perpetua.

65 (Upper) JOHN DAY RIVER . . . Colorful and symmetrical Sheep Mountain towers above the John Day River in Eastern Oregon. This region is famed for the fossils which are found in this area of Oregon.

(Lower) WALLOWA LAKE . . . Thunderheads billow above Wallowa Valley in northeastern Oregon. Wallowa Lake in the middle distance was created by glacier moraines that dwarf the size of many man-made dams. The photograph was taken from Mt. Howard in the Wallowa Range.

66

(Upper) GRANDE RONDE VALLEY ... Timbered and grassy slopes of Oregon's Blue Mountains sweep down from Mt. Emily toward La Grande on the western edge of the rich Grande Ronde Valley in northeastern Oregon.

(Lower) OWYHEE RIVER ... The Owyhee River has carved its way through a couple of hundred miles of the most colorful and spectacular geography in the Pacific Northwest. Here is a scene at Whistling Bird Camp where a boating party has pulled in for rest and exploration during a "run" of the river.

(Right) JOHN DAY VALLEY ... Autumn has waved its magic wand over eastern Oregon, sprinkling the lofty peak of Strawberry Mountain with a light coat of snow and creating a kaleidoscope of color in the foliage of picturesque John Day Valley.

68 (Upper) SMITH ROCKS STATE PARK . . . The Crooked River winds through Smith Rocks State Park in Central Oregon. Snow-crowned peaks of the Cascade Range dominate the skyline.
(Lower) PAINTED HILLS STATE PARK . . . Fluffy summertime clouds float lazily above the erosion of Oregon's Painted Hills State Park.

70   (Upper Left) IMNAHA RIVER CANYON . . . Rugged canyons and rolling hills are features of the wild Imnaha River canyon in northeastern Oregon. Fertile farmland lines the flatland along the side of the river. The slopes and high plateaus above serve as rangeland for cattle and sheep ranches.

  (Lower) FOREE FOSSIL BEDS . . . Layers of earth and stone alternate in the Foree area of the John Day Valley, where many spectacular fossil finds have occurred.

  (Upper Right) ANTHONY LAKES SKI AREA . . . A skier speeds down a slope of new snow on the crest of Oregon's Blue Mountains in the Anthony Lakes area.

  (Right) WALLOWA MOUNTAINS . . . Horses and riders pass along a lake shore in the Wallowa Mountains of eastern Oregon, the 'Alps' of America.